0901900

ON LINE

JBIOG
Garne
Edwards, Ethan

**Meet Kevin Garnett : basketball's
big ticket**

All-Star Players™

MEET
KEVIN
GARNETT

Basketball's Big Ticket

Ethan Edwards

PowerKiDS press™

New York

Published in 2009 by The Rosen Publishing Group, Inc.
29 East 21st Street, New York, NY 10010

First Edition

Editor: Amelie von Zumbusch
Book Design: Greg Tucker
Photo Researcher: Jessica Gerweck

Photo Credits: Cover, pp. 4, 10, 12, 13, 15, 16, 17, 18, 20, 21, 22, 25, 29, 30 © Getty Images; pp. 7, 26 © NBAE/Getty Images; p. 8 © Icon Sports Media; p. 27 © WireImage.

Library of Congress Cataloging-in-Publication Data

Edwards, Ethan.
  Meet Kevin Garnett : basketball's big ticket / Ethan Edwards. — 1st ed.
       p. cm. — (All-star players)
  Includes index.
  ISBN 978-1-4042-4490-0 (library binding)
  1. Garnett, Kevin, 1976– —Juvenile literature. 2. Basketball players—United States—Biography—Juvenile literature. I. Title.
  GV884.G37E39 2009
  796.323092—dc22
  [B]
                                            2008003489

Manufactured in the United States of America

02/2009
AB
$23.95

Contents

Kevin Garnett (right) is one of today's most skilled basketball players.

Meet Kevin Garnett

Kevin Garnett is one of the most **versatile** players in the NBA, or National Basketball Association. Garnett plays a position called forward. There are two kinds of forwards, small forwards and power forwards. Garnett can play both positions. He is also good at playing the center position. This is what makes him so versatile.

Do not be fooled by the term small forward. There is nothing small about Garnett. He stands 6 feet 11 inches (2.1 m) tall! However, there are lots of tall people who never become basketball stars. Garnett is a star because he loves hard work, teamwork, and basketball.

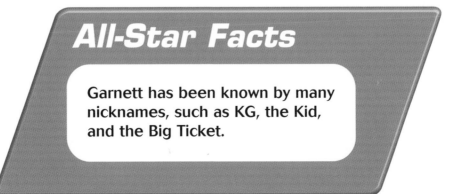

All-Star Facts

Garnett has been known by many nicknames, such as KG, the Kid, and the Big Ticket.

Garnett grew up in a small town, called Mauldin, in South Carolina. He became a basketball fan at a very young age. His **idol** was the famous basketball player Magic Johnson.

Garnett knew that he was lucky to be tall. However, he also knew that being tall was not enough. It would take lots of hard work and practice in order to play **professional** basketball. Garnett used to sneak out of his bedroom window in the middle of the night to practice on a neighborhood playground. The practice paid off, and Garnett became the star of his high-school basketball team.

All-Star Facts

Garnett loved the Ramona books, a series by Beverly Cleary, when he was growing up.

In time, Garnett (back) got the chance to play against his hero, Magic Johnson (front).

Mr. Basketball

Garnett and his family moved to Chicago, Illinois, for Garnett's final year of high school. He attended Farragut Career Academy. Farragut had an excellent basketball program, and Garnett soon became famous. The state of Illinois named him Mr. Basketball. The newspaper *USA Today* wrote that Garnett was the best high-school basketball player in the nation.

Garnett was so good that **scouts** from the NBA attended his games to watch him play. Even the best basketball players generally need to play in college before they are ready for the NBA. However, Garnett did not need to play in college. He was good enough for the NBA at the age of 18!

When Garnett (right) played for the Farragut Academy Admirals in his last year of high school, he averaged more than 25 points a game.

The Minnesota Timberwolves

Garnett tried out for the NBA by entering the 1995 NBA Draft. The draft is a system in which each team gets the chance to select the best young players. The Minnesota Timberwolves picked Garnett in the draft's first round.

The Timberwolves were a new team, and they were not very good. The Timberwolves' management was looking for an excellent young player who could be a team leader. Garnett was exactly what they were looking for. He was a big, strong **defensive** player who could fill several **roles** on the team.

Garnett did not play as a starter for the first half of his **rookie** season. Instead, he came off the

Garnett was the first major-league basketball player in over 20 years to be drafted straight out of high school.

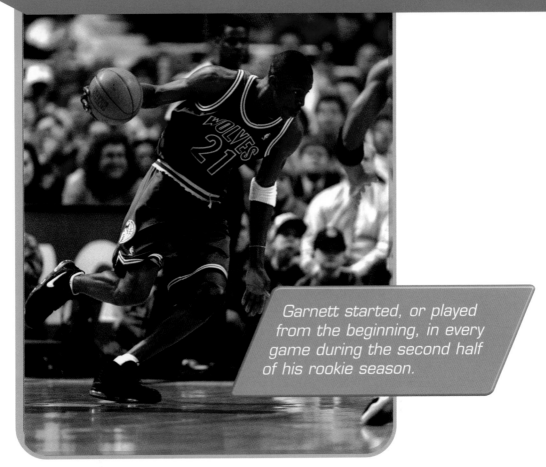

Garnett started, or played from the beginning, in every game during the second half of his rookie season.

bench to relieve the **veterans**. Then, the Timberwolves fired their coach in the middle of the season. They hired a new coach, Phil "Flip" Saunders. Saunders realized that Garnett was already one of the best players on the team. He decided to play him as much as possible.

The Timberwolves finished the season with a losing record, but it was still their best record so far. Garnett was already on his way to becoming a star. Minnesota fans finally had reason to be happy. It was not bad for his first season!

Although he was just 19, Garnett was one of the Timberwolves' best players during the 1995–1996 season.

Garnett played so well that the Timberwolves offered him $126 million in just his third season. Basketball **experts** thought this was crazy. However, Garnett soon showed them that he was worth every penny.

The Timberwolves finished the 1997–1998 season with their first winning record. Garnett led them to the **play-offs** for the second season in a row. Unfortunately, the Timberwolves lost in the first round to the Seattle Supersonics.

People soon began calling Garnett the **Franchise**. He got this nickname because he carried his team. Garnett inspired the other Timberwolves to play better. His hard work rubbed off on them.

All-Star Facts

In 2000, Garnett joined other American basketball stars to play on the U.S. Olympic team. They won the gold medal, or first place.

During the 1997–1998 season, Garnett was named NBA Player of the Month once and Player of the Week three times.

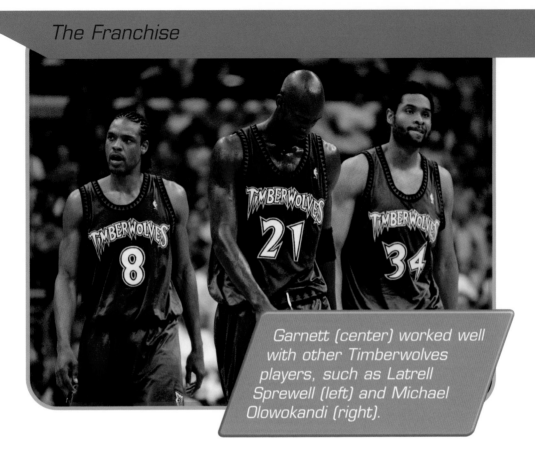

Garnett (center) worked well with other Timberwolves players, such as Latrell Sprewell (left) and Michael Olowokandi (right).

In 2003, promising young players Latrell Sprewell and Sam Cassell joined the team. They played well with Garnett, and the Timberwolves became one of the NBA's best teams. Sprewell and Cassell became stars in their own right, but Garnett shone even more brightly. In 2004, basketball **journalists** voted Garnett the Most Valuable Player, or MVP. The MVP is the player who does more for his team than any other player in basketball.

The Timberwolves made the play-offs almost every year after Garnett joined the team. Unfortunately, the team kept losing in the early rounds. Would Garnett ever win a championship?

Garnett proudly showed off his MVP trophy, or award, during the 2004 NBA play-offs.

Though his team struggled, Garnett continued to play well. By 2007, he had scored more points than any other Timberwolves player ever had.

Down in the Dumps

In 2004, things began to fall apart for the Timberwolves. Garnett had an excellent season, but the team played poorly. The Timberwolves failed to make the play-offs for the first time in eight years. Sprewell and Cassell were unhappy with the poor play of the team, and they left during the 2005–2006 season.

Garnett was often **frustrated** with his team's poor play because he felt he was working harder than the others. He continued to play well despite the team's overall performance. However, Garnett learned that he could not do everything by himself. The Timberwolves continued to struggle into 2007.

All-Star Facts

In 2004, Garnett became the fifth-youngest player in NBA history to score more than 13,000 points.

In 2007, the team's management decided to build a team around young players. This meant the team would not be able to afford Garnett. The management decided to trade him.

Garnett did not want to join a different team.

One reason that Garnett is such a wonderful player is that he is very good at blocking other players.

He liked playing for the Timberwolves even if they were a bad team. Garnett became known as one of the most **loyal** basketball players of all time.

The Timberwolves wanted lots of talent in exchange for Garnett. Many teams were interested in getting the Franchise, but not all of them had enough money or players to trade.

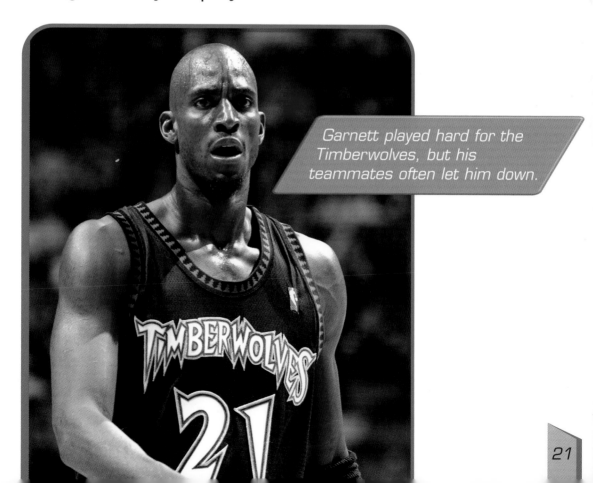

Garnett played hard for the Timberwolves, but his teammates often let him down.

The Boston Celtics

The Boston Celtics wanted Garnett badly. The Celtics are a team with a rich basketball history. They were one of the best teams in the 1980s. However, they did not play well in the early 2000s. The owners of the Celtics wanted to bring a championship back to Boston. They decided to build a team of superstars.

The Celtics wanted Garnett so badly that they offered to trade the Timberwolves seven players for him! It was one of the biggest single-player trades of all time. Garnett joined the Celtics for the 2007–2008 season. Garnett was excited to play for the Celtics. He believed he could help the team win an NBA championship.

The Celtics and Garnett (right) won eight games in a row at the start of the 2007–2008 season.

Kevin Garnett lives in Concord, Massachusetts, with his wife, Brandi Padilla. The pair met through Garnett's friend, the record producer Jimmy Jam Harris. Harris's wife is Brandi Padilla's sister.

Athleticism runs in Garnett's family. His half brother Louis McCullough plays basketball for the Syracuse Raging Bullz. His cousin Shammond Williams played for the Los Angeles Lakers.

Basketball is important to Garnett, but he knows there are more important things in the world. In 2005, Hurricane Katrina hit the state of Louisiana. The hurricane created floods that swept

All-Star Facts

Garnett appeared in the movie *Rebound*, as the great basketball player Wilt Chamberlain.

Garnett married his long-time girlfriend, Brandi Padilla, in the summer of 2004.

In September 2005, Garnett visited people who were driven from their homes by Hurricane Katrina.

through the city of New Orleans. Many people died. Lots of families lost their homes. Garnett watched the hurricane on the news. He felt awful for the homeless families. Garnett **donated** more than $1 million to help New Orleans families build new homes. His money built one home a month for two years. Garnett received the J. Walter Kennedy Citizenship Award for giving so much money.

Garnett also feels strongly about helping young people achieve their goals. He knows that not everyone is lucky enough to be a basketball star. Garnett teamed up with business leaders at Monster.com to create a program, called 4XL-For Excellence in Leadership. 4XL brings high-school and college students and business leaders together. It helps students become the leaders of the future.

In 2007, Garnett took part in football player Matt Leinart's first Celebrity Bowling Night. This event raised money to support kids.

Garnett is no longer called the Franchise. His new teammates Paul Pierce and Ray Allen are also superstars. Garnett, Pierce, and Allen are now called the Big Three. Garnett no longer has to carry the team all by himself. He has lots of help. The Celtics are one of the best teams in the NBA.

Garnett used to watch Magic Johnson and dream of playing in the NBA. Now Garnett is the idol of future basketball stars. He is also the idol of the families and students he helps. Hopefully, Garnett will continue to inspire fans with his hard work, his good deeds, and his love of basketball for many years to come.

His skill and many years of hard work have made Kevin Garnett one of the very best players in the NBA.

Height: 6' 11" (2.1 m)
Weight: 220 pounds (100 kg)
Team: Boston Celtics
Position: Power forward, small
                   forward, or center
Uniform Number: 5
Date of Birth: May 19, 1976

2006–2007 Season Stats

Games Played	3-Point Percentage	Free-Throw Percentage	Rebounds per Game	Assists per Game	Points per Game
76	.214	.835	12.8	4.1	22.4

NBA Career Stats as of Summer 2007

Games Played	3-Point Percentage	Free-Throw Percentage	Rebounds per Game	Assists per Game	Points per Game
927	.27	.77	11.33	4.46	20.53

Glossary

athleticism (ath-LEH-tuh-sih-zum) Ability and training in sports and exercises of strength.

defensive (dih-FEN-siv) Playing in a position that tries to prevent the other team from scoring.

donated (DOH-nayt-ed) Gave something away.

experts (EK-sperts) People who know a lot about a subject.

franchise (FRAN-chyz) A professional sports team.

frustrated (FRUS-trayt-ed) Upset.

idol (EYE-dul) Someone whom many people look up to.

journalists (JER-nul-ists) People who gather and write news for newspapers or magazines.

loyal (LOY-ul) Faithful to a person or an idea.

play-offs (PLAY-ofs) Games played after the regular season ends to see who will play in the championship game.

professional (pruh-FESH-nul) Having to do with someone who is paid for what he or she does.

roles (ROHLZ) Parts played by people or things.

rookie (RU-kee) A new major-league player.

scouts (SKOWTS) People who help sports teams find new, young players.

versatile (VER-suh-tul) Able to do many different things well.

veterans (VEH-tuh-runz) People who have had their jobs for a long time.

Index

Web Sites

Due to the changing nature of Internet links, PowerKids Press has developed an online list of Web sites related to the subject of this book. This site is updated regularly. Please use this link to access the list:
www.powerkidslinks.com/asp/garnett/